3/95

D'Arcy McNickle

By James Ruppert
University of Alaska–Fairbanks

Editors: Wayne Chatterton
James H. Maguire

Business Manager:
James Hadden

Cover Design and Illustration
by Arny Skov, Copyright 1988

Boise State University, Boise, Idaho

The author gratefully acknowledges the support provided by a grant from the Newberry Library and by a Travel to Collections grant from the National Endowment for the Humanities.

Printed in the United States of America by
Boise State University Printing and Graphics Services
Boise, Idaho

D'Arcy McNickle

D'Arcy McNickle

I. BIOGRAPHY

A man of many talents, D'Arcy McNickle was noted as a public official, historian, Indian Rights advocate, and novelist. Through his writing and years of tireless public and personal service, McNickle influenced the history of white/Indian interaction, an interaction which was the focus of his energies and intellect. Today many scholars consider him to be the grandfather of Modern Native American Literature and Modern Native American Ethnohistory.

In his novel *The Surrounded*, McNickle described the Montana landscape of his birth:

> Northward, the eye traveled up a pleasant valley for fifty miles below the haze and a gradually ascending tableland blurred on the horizon. A stranger would not have suspected that just beyond lay a great lake, a mirror to the sky for forty miles. But the most startling vision were the mountains. Without foothills, though with curving approaches which spread some distance out upon the valley floor, the mountains raised a magnificent barricade against the eastern sky, the highest jagged crests floating in morning mist 8000 feet above the valley. One felt humbled and contrite. (43-44)

Into this haunting land, William D'Arcy McNickle was born on 18 January 1904 at St. Ignatius, Montana. His mother Philomena Parenteau, of Cree descent but adopted into the Flathead tribe, had married Irish rancher William McNickle and lived with him on the reservation. The Parenteaus had come to the reservation shortly after the aborted Metis uprising of 1885. D'Arcy's grandfather Isidore Parenteau had fought with Louis Riel. After the defeat of the Metis, Isidore gathered his family and fled across the border to the Flathead reservation where he was taken in. Though Isidore was eventually pardoned and returned to Canada in 1910, his daughter chose to remain with her husband and her adopted Flathead tribe in Montana.

D'Arcy spent his early years on the reservation living a life that placed him in proximity to the Flatheads, but never let him really become part of them. As was common for the day, his parents felt he would be better off if he were encouraged to develop an identification with white society rather than tie himself to the cycle of despair and poverty that characterized early twentieth-century reservations. In a letter much later in life, he wrote: "My recollection of that period in my own life is that we knew so little and tried to ignore what we did not know, since it was not a source of pride. . . . As 'breeds' we could not turn for reassurance to an Indian tradition, and certainly not to the white community" (Letter to Karen Fenton, 15 October 1974). Yet young D'Arcy was always sneaking out to play with the young Salish children, developing a strong attachment to the Indian people and culture there. Though he never went back to the reservation to live after he left in 1925, his writing—especially his fiction—was firmly rooted there. Helen L. Peterson, a friend and long-time ally in Indian Affairs work remembered D'Arcy saying that "he entered school when he was eleven years old, wearing long hair in the Indian tradition, and speaking no English [probably, he spoke French]" (Letter to Omer Stewart, 28 January 1966).

Against McNickle's and his mother's desires, he was sent away, probably in 1915, to the Chemawa Indian School in Oregon. His boarding school experiences were similar to those of other Indian youths. The school was permeated with the oppression and intolerance exhibited by teachers convinced of their moral superiority. His negative experiences were only partially balanced by a love of music he learned at Chemawa. As presented in his highly autobiographical novel *The Surrounded*, the clash of values inherent in the boarding schools tended to crush the spirit and too often the life out of young Indian students. After three years at the school, he attended public school in Washington and Montana.

At the age of seventeen, he left the reservation for the University of Montana. There he found himself drawn to literature and languages, including Greek and Latin. As the realm of literature opened up to him, he forgot the confinement of the boarding school and the reservation and dedicated himself to contributing to literature's timeless and raceless world. He wrote fiction, drama, and especially poetry, winning the notice of some of the professors at the university as well as winning a statewide poetry contest held by the *Daily Missoulian*. Eventually he was suspended from school for skipping too many classes during which he spent his time in the library reading and writing poetry.

After three and a half years at the university, his mentor, Professor Meriam, convinced him to go to Oxford to finish his degree rather than return to the University of Montana. Meriam wrote a strong letter of recommendation which resulted in McNickle's admission. McNickle sold the allotment of land near St. Ignatius which he had received as a member of the Flathead tribe, and enthusiastically headed off for England in 1925. He spent most of a year there, but he found that the university officials would not accept most of his credits; consequently, he would need to stay at least two years. He stayed as long as his money held out, but in 1926, he moved to Paris with vague ideas of being a writer and musician.

He was a young man, unsure of his calling in life, but after falling in with a crowd of dedicated, semi-professional musicians, he became convinced that he should stick with writing. However, he thought that for an American writer, New York was still the place to be discovered and to make some money, so he set off for it. "I knew that I wanted to write and that I did not want to return to the scenes from which I had fled. What exactly was on my mind on that May morning in 1926 when I returned from Paris, I cannot now recall" (diary 11 August 1932).

Unfortunately, when he arrived at New York the only job McNickle could find was selling automobiles. He grudgingly allowed himself to be taught the high-pressure sales techniques through which he saw America playing out its certainty that corporations and consumerism would produce a materialistic paradise on earth. "In my first job selling automobiles, I went through seven months' daily betrayal of my birthright in opposition. Everything I was called upon to do was a violation of instinct and desire" (diary 11 August 1932). He felt an instinctive distrust of capitalistic enterprise and conventional business morality, a distrust which he termed his sense of "opposition." As with other intellectuals of the day, he could see no creative and humanistic achievement growing out of this money ethic.

From 1927 to 1935, McNickle labored in a variety of editorial and professional jobs while he tried to sell his novel, short stories, and poetry. From 1927 to 1928, he worked on the staff of the Encyclopaedia Britannica under Walter B. Pitkin, and then he moved to Philadelphia to work with trade journals published by E.F. Houghton. From 1928 to 1934, he was back in New York employed as editor by the National Cyclopaedia of American Biography. In 1931 he left work to attend the University of Grenoble for a semester, returning to New York afterward. While in New York, he periodically attended courses at the New School for Social Research and at Columbia University.

During this period, McNickle seems to have had little contact with the reservation and with his family. When D'Arcy was young, his mother had divorced his father and married August Dahlberg. In 1932, he had so completely lost track of his mother, that in writing to the Superintendent of the reservation to ask about his tribal annuities, he also requested her address. Until 1933, however, he went under the name of D'Arcy Dahlberg at the request of his mother. With the birth of his daughter approaching in 1933, he decided that he wanted to perpetuate the name of McNickle and began to go by that name.

McNickle later refers to these New York years from 1927 to 1934 as "a confusion," when he felt he was "in opposition" but uncertain to what exactly. Like many of the young intellectuals of the "Lost Generation" of a few years previous, he was struggling against a changing society that seemed soulless and unaware of its own possibilities. He was, however, vitally involved with the intellectual and artistic life of New York in those years from before the stockmarket crash to the first part of the Great Depression, attending the theater, listening constantly to classical music, arguing literature, attending lectures, passionately discussing politics, especially the election of Roosevelt and the chances of the socialists, and developing his taste for good wine and penetrating conversation. Some of his unpublished short stories deal with his life during those years, though his heart still seemed to lie with writing about the real West.

When he left the Cyclopaedia in 1934, he briefly worked as a manuscript reader while trying to write full-time. But marriage and a new daughter forced him to push for the security of full-time employment. Later that year, he was so broke that he couldn't pay his 1933 income taxes of $23 and had to get an extension. After reading about a plan whereby the Office of Indian Affairs under the newly appointed commissioner John Collier was planning on hiring qualified Indians to work in the Indian Office, McNickle applied, but the wheels of bureaucracy turned as slowly as they always have. Though he applied in May of 1934, the Office did not know where it could use him, and it waited for its congressional appropriation. In early 1935, he could wait no longer for them and accepted a staff position with the Federal Writers Project. A year later, in March of 1936, the position with the Indian office came through, and Collier wrote to tell him to come to the department as an administrative assistant.

In 1936, his first novel, *The Surrounded*, was published. Early drafts of the novel had been circulating with New York publishers since 1927, but while many of their reactions were favorable, none would take a chance on it. After many revisions of the manuscript, Dodd finally published it. When it came out, the reviews were very positive. Many critics such as Oliver La Farge praised the balance of an "excellent story" with significant background, and they appreciated his style: "The writing is simple, clear, direct, devoid of affectations, and fast moving" (10). La Farge went so far as to place the book on the "small list of creditable modern novels using the first Americans as theme."

In the Depression-dominated book market, however, *The Surrounded* did not sell well. In the first six months it sold 624 copies, but after that sales dropped off to almost nothing. McNickle probably made only $100 from it. Nevertheless, he was encouraged to keep writing. He began to draw some notice from other publishers and writers such as Constance Lindsay Skinner who suggested writing projects.

McNickle's career with the Bureau of Indian Affairs (BIA) lasted sixteen years. He began as an assistant to Collier, but later took up the post of field representative and then director of tribal relations. His jobs varied widely from census work to attempts to create new reservations for landless Indians, from structuring tribal councils to initiating tribal courts, and from fighting for Pima water rights to working during World War II on a cooperative project with the War Relocation Authority to place relocated Japanese on a reservation at Poston, Arizona.

McNickle's interest in Indian affairs widened when in 1940 he served as an American representative to the Inter-American conference on Indian life organized by Collier, Oliver La Farge, and Mexican social scientists. In 1944, because he was convinced that tribes could not depend on reformist associations or government agencies and must therefore unite on a national political level in order to protect their rights, he co-founded the National Congress of American Indians (NCAI).

In the BIA, McNickle found a clear direction that replaced the New York years of confusion. As he faced the problems and despair which he had fled, he found a purpose and a vehicle. Collier offered McNickle a way to help countless Indians from backgrounds similar to his to fight the despair and still remain Indian. A broad understanding of the cultural clash gave McNickle a historical framework from which to view his own life. He could act directly, though hampered by a bureaucracy which was occasionally sympathetic but seldom understanding. In a late letter mentioning a book he had read at Oxford which expressed Bacon's attitude toward Indians, he recalled that when reading it, "Bacon's attitude toward Indians escaped me entirely, but that was a long time ago when I wasn't looking for the enemy" (Letter to Wilcomb Washburn, 22 August 1973). In the BIA, he learned to see the enemy, one he recognized from his childhood—racial intolerance, cultural superiority, and genocide.

His years with the BIA were also full of publishing activity. He made numerous addresses and published several articles and short stories, but his major accomplishment was the creation of his ground-breaking contribution to ethnohistory. In 1949 he published *They Came Here First: The Epic of the American Indian,* a history that drew heavily on anthropological sources and his personal work-related research in the National Archives to present a complete vision of white/Indian relations. He always regretted that he was unable to write more fiction during those years, but his work at the BIA and on non-fiction was important, and this writing was "more or less in the line of duty."

Under ever-increasing attack through the early 1940s, Collier resigned in 1945. McNickle remained with the BIA and attempted to defend and continue to implement a number of Collier's reforms as they related to community organizing. As he characterized the political climate at the time of Collier's departure and thereafter, the "wolves were in the land." But by 1952 with a new commissioner and a Congress calling for termination and relocation, McNickle felt he could do no more. He decided to take a leave of absence from the Bureau, officially resigning in 1954. His last position with the BIA concerned overseeing financial self-help programs and a revolving credit fund. Given a government climate that was unwilling to support self-help programs, he was convinced that he could be of more service to the tribes if some private organization were set up to direct private money into programs which emphasized development and self-determination at the community level.

Through its tax-deductible affiliate organization, Arrow, Inc., the NCAI created American Indian Development, Inc. (AID), and McNickle served as its director. With Boulder, Colorado, as its home base, AID sought private funds to finance leadership training and group development in Indian communities. While AID worked with many groups like the Eastern Cherokee, its most lasting involvement was with the community of Crownpoint, New Mexico, where it organized health and citizen education projects as well as the construction of a community house. McNickle saw this as a "serious program of research and action in the field," but it clearly was a social program with a difference—besides its attempt to act from an Indian perspective, AID also was dedicated to providing no assistance unless it was specifically requested by local people.

During the fifties while D'Arcy McNickle was deeply committed to community projects, he also hit his stride as a writer and scholar. He published many articles and two books. In 1954, *Runner in the Sun: A Story of Indian Maize* was published as a part of a series of juvenile historical novels. Set in the pre-Columbian Southwest, the story told of a boy, Salt, who made a dangerous journey to the opulent Aztec cities to find a new strain of corn, but instead brought back new knowledge to aid his people. Together with social journalist Harold Fey, McNickle authored *Indians and Other Americans: Two Ways of Life Meet.* The book attempted to answer the question raised by the authors in their first chapter: "Why has failure so clouded white/Indian relations?" Its review of the mistakes of federal Indian policy prepared the ground for a defense of Collier's cultural relativist reforms and an attack on the policies of the post-war Eisenhower years.

McNickle's dedication and intellectual energy did not go unnoticed by those around him. In 1954 he was appointed a visiting lecturer at Regis College in Denver. In 1955 he received a citation from the National Congress of American Indians for distinguished service to Native Americans. He felt honored to serve as a member on the U.S. Civil Rights Commission, and felt that one of the most significant honors that had come his way was to be asked to serve on the Fellowship Awards Committee of the John Whitney Hay Foundation. From 1957 to 1971, he was able to help Indian students find funds for education. In the sixties he was awarded a Guggenheim Fellowship so that he could work on a long overdue book-length report on his Crownpoint community development activities as well as on his fiction and some articles.

The sixties proved to be an equally active decade for McNickle. In 1961, he was involved with a conference of Indian tribal leaders at the University of Chicago and was instrumental in creating a conference statement called "A Declaration of Indian Purpose." In it the leaders called for material assistance for Indian communities and moral support for cultural self-determination. Both McNickle and the tribal leaders saw some hope in the promise of the new Kennedy administration.

Throughout the sixties, he was encouraged by the increased political awareness of Indians and about Indian tribes. He continued to organize the Workshop on Indian Affairs, which he had helped found in 1956 as a summer leadership workshop for Indian college students. He was confident that his work with NCAI, AID, and the Workshop had some positive influence. As he wrote to Royal Hassrick, president of AID, "Students from the Workshop are busy changing the image of Indians in the general population. It is with astonishment that I look up at times and realize what changes have struck the climate in which Indian affairs are discussed. I believe we contributed something to that" (16 March 1969).

In 1966 academia found him. The University of Colorado gave him an honorary doctorate, and the University of Saskatchewan made him an offer that he could not turn down: he accepted a full professorship and chairman responsibilities to set up and staff a small anthropology department at the new Regina campus.

He also continued his work as a scholar and author during those years. In 1962 Oxford University Press published his *Indian Tribes of the United States*. He took the 1968-69 academic year off to finish his biography of Oliver La Farge, the writer, anthropologist, and Indian rights activist who had headed the Association on American Indian Affairs for many years. When, in 1971, Indiana University Press finally brought the biography out as *Indian Man: A Life of Oliver La Farge*, it was nominated for a National Book Award. During the late sixties, he also served on the editorial board for the Smithsonian Institution's revision of the *Handbook of North American Indians.*

When he retired in 1971 to Albuquerque, dozens of writing projects lay stacked on his desk. He was happy to leave academia: as he wrote to Michael Harrison, "Academic life turned out to be a greater bureaucratic trap than the BIA and I was glad to be out of it" (18 December 1971). However, his scholarly retreat was interrupted in 1972 when he was asked to become the founding director of the Newberry Library's Center for the History of the American Indian. McNickle agreed. As he traveled back and forth between Albuquerque and Chicago, he helped gather support for the project. One of his prime goals for the center was that it should be able to offer fellowships to young scholars, especially Indian scholars, as well as to archive valuable material. Upon his death the center was named after him.

During his final years, he revised two of his books and prepared his last novel, *Wind from an Enemy Sky*, for publication. He was constantly in demand for many consulting and writing assignments that he could not possibly take on. In October of 1977, he died in Albuquerque of a massive coronary.

II. FICTION

The years between 1927 and 1937 were McNickle's most productive years for literature. Although he was forced to remain at a full-time job, writing only in his spare time, he was quite productive. He wrote and rewrote one novel and began a second. He completed dozens of short stories and poems, though he sold only a few. He was completely involved with the intellectual life of the city and wrote some short stories dealing with experiences in New York and Paris, but his best developed and most vital stories explored characters and situations which grew out of his boyhood in Montana.

McNickle was not, however, interested in writing about the West in what he called the romantic vein. Rather he was interested in revealing the Western character as it was formed by the impact of the frontier upon the lives of the people who settled it as revealed by historical writers and his experiences as a youth. His stories are peopled with tired trappers, misled ranchers, amiable but ineffectual Indian agents, and loyal but unyielding shop keepers who will not change with the times: characters reminiscent of the farmers in stories by Hamlin Garland, the trappers in works by Jack London and by Southern regionalists, narratives in which man struggles in a harsh land and is not bathed in the pure light of nature.

I am writing of the West, not of Indians primarily, and certainly not of the romantic West which best-selling authors have exploited to the detriment of a rational understanding of the meaning of the West, the Frontier, in American life. I have chosen the medium of fiction, first of all because I understand the story-telling art, and in the second place I know by rationalization that fiction reaches a wider audience than any other form of writing; and if it is good fiction it should tell a man as much about himself as a text combining something of philosophy, psychology, a little physiology, and some history, and should at the same time please his esthetic sense, stir his emotions, and send him off with the will to make use of his best quality, which is his understanding. (Letter to John Collier, Exhibit C, 4 May 1934)

Primarily, his work reveals a dedication to character in a realistic setting, not simply in the manner of the local colorists, but rather as a regionalist who wants to understand how the values that people hold and the clash of those values, whether intra- or inter-cultural, rise out of the land. His characters are developed more from what they believe and are brought up to believe as members of human groups than from individual psychology.

McNickle's fiction is not easily grouped with the expansive, epic, land-oriented novels of rugged individualism, an individualism that regionalist scholars like John Milton say is the center of the traditional Western novel. Yet McNickle's characters do exhibit many of the qualities that Milton outlines, of historical awareness and attempted moral action as opposed to psychological motivation. While his characters are shaped more by culture than the land, a quality Milton associates with Eastern novels, it is clearly Western cultures that interest McNickle. The bond with the land that his characters exhibit is at the center of their perceptions and so completely ingrained into their attitudes that McNickle sees it expressed not in mythic emotions of harmony and rebirth, but in culturally sanctioned behaviors and values. The portrayal of the Indians in both *The Surrounded* and *Wind from an Enemy Sky* emphasizes the Western landscape as an expression of their culture, links their freedom with its openness, its destruction with their own. Their communion with the land is through hunts, moving camps, and ritual action, rather than moments of mystic unity.

Milton argues that three turn-of-the-century books form the foundation of the twentieth-century Western American novel: Owen Wister's *The Virginian*, the popular western novel, the cowboy novel; Frank Norris' *The Octopus*, a juxtaposition of Naturalism and Romanticism, and Mary Austin's *The Land of Little Rain*, an expression of the spiritual penetration of the harmonies of the Western landscape. Clearly, McNickle draws more from the Norris tradition than from Austin or Wister.

Perhaps his work is best understood if McNickle is considered as a regionalist with a Naturalist's goals. While definitions of regionalism vary, essential to McNickle's regionalism is an understanding of culture as a system of values held by a people. McNickle's regionalism, while tied to the land as all regionalist work is, seeks to explore the individual in his environmental context, "the character which was formed by the impact of the Frontier upon the lives of the people who settled it" (Letter to John Collier, 4 May 1934), and especially the experience of the American Indian. As in works by Hamlin Garland, Katharine Anne Porter, Willa Cather, and other regionalists, the emphasis is on how the belief systems of regional groups define and express character rather than on how the West frees individuals from social restraints.

The Surrounded

As many first novels are, *The Surrounded* (1936) is highly autobiographical. The protagonist, young Archilde Leon, experiences much of the same clash of cultural values and expectations that young McNickle did. He has left the reservation and grown alienated from his people and their way of life. The white boarding school and the white society have convinced him that there is nothing of value, nothing modern and progressive, existing on the reservation, yet he is drawn back to it by the quality of experience there.

18

He yearns for some fulfillment, a fullness of culture welded to the surrounding, nurturing valley of his youth, a cultural wholeness that he senses is lacking in the white world. During what he considers to be his final visit back home, Archilde becomes entrapped in the problems of his family and his people. Through a tragic series of misunderstandings and mismatched cultural expectations, he is brought to ruin.

The novel owes much to the Naturalistic tradition in American literature. As in the works of Theodore Dreiser and Frank Norris, the forces that work on Archilde tend to encircle and ensnare him. He is a product of his environment, and those conflicting values which characterize his environment as a half-breed torn between the reservation life and modern white life, structure his dilemma and eventual tragedy. At moments both the reader and Archilde feel his fate is out of his hands.

However, as in works of American Naturalism, the novel strives to express insights about man's lack of efficacy and thus lack of responsibility for his fate, and it also refuses to accept this denial as the total meaning of life, and thus seeks a new basis for dignity and importance, one that is opposed to nineteenth-century romanticized concepts of meaning and value. McNickle's primary goal in *The Surrounded* is not solely to demonstrate the overwhelming power of the environmental forces on people's lives, but to show the intermingling of those forces in personal actions which reveal the individual's and group's worth. Consequently, the novel attempts to show a modified appreciation of human value while it tries to destroy outmoded and culture-locked sources of value and human importance. While its bleak view of human potential and cross-cultural interaction can not be denied, as in all naturalist novels, man's weaknesses, limited knowledge, and thwarted desires are still sources of compassion and worth. Archilde is a worthy quester and questioner who searches for life-sustaining values, and this quality ennobles him, not the easy success of the culture hero or any sociological solution. His struggle and volition may not be effective, but they create value. In this novel, ultimate success is not the measure of human worth, rather it is the struggle against environmental forces that redeems man.

Ultimately, McNickle's cross-cultural insights enliven the Naturalistic tradition: as a regionalist, his understanding of culture enriches the naturalistic framework in a manner of which turn-of-the-century naturalists were not capable. Though he presents social problems on and around the reservation, McNickle is more interested in exploring the mismatched understanding the two peoples have of each other than in analyzing any one problem. He writes, "I was not at the time of writing, aware of the social science implications of the scene I was describing. If I had tried to state a theme it would have had to do with the clash of values, of which I had been aware from earliest childhood" (Letter to Priscilla Oakes, 10 June 1973).

To highlight this clash, the novel employs a parallel structure. Incidents that happen to Archilde in one society are paralleled by actions in the other. There are two communities, Indian and white; two dances, one at the Farmers Hall and one Indian ceremonial dance; two religions, traditional Indian and Catholic; two types of education, BIA boarding school and traditional Indian personal instruction. Two old men want to lead Archilde, Modeste and Grepilloux. Each sees in him a hope for the future. Archilde takes two trips into the fateful mountains, one with his mother and one with Elise. Two ages inform the story, the primitive one during which the Indians still maintained some control over their lives, even if the missionaries were there, and the modern one when progress has created confusion and sadness. Archilde is enlightened

20

by two major stories of the past, one recorded by the Jesuits who first came to the valley, the other an oral story told by Modeste. Archilde's farm has two houses, one for each parent, and ultimately, Archilde's life is formed by two parents.

Archilde's family is literally a marriage of cultures as McNickle's was. Archilde's father is Spanish and his mother is Salish. Although they have five children together, they have never really understood each other nor each other's values. The mother has been a model Christian on the outside, but inside, has maintained an Indian understanding of life. The father could never understand why his wife's people couldn't make the fertile soil pay off through hard work. After years of sniping at each other, the two live in houses that are separate but near. The marriage is in complete decay and despair, and so are the relations between white and Indian cultures. As death approaches, each parent has an epiphany. The father understands that years of white material progress have not brought happiness to the Indians, and the mother, deciding her Christianity is a lie, goes back to the old religion. But fate cuts off the hope offered by these new understandings as both characters die.

McNickle makes it clear that the communal and social strength of the Salish people has been sapped by the white reservation system. Also partly to blame is the Indian's own subservient, fatalistic attitude toward the powerful white priests. The forces of white society have individualized the tribe, broken them apart so that no cultural dynamic is present. The characters who represent the forces of the status quo are isolated and demoralized while those who represent the forces of change either move away or come to express their hopeless despair through self-destructive abandon. McNickle portrays this as the true death of a culture, when the vital social organization and dynamic interaction are missing.

Archilde does not want to abandon his Indian world, but he feels he must if he is ever to have a future. He knows he can not ignore the present breakdown and go back to an idyllic past that no longer exists, and he sees no way to remedy the massive destruction around him. Even for a half-breed, there seems to be no way to stay in both worlds; each calls for a repudiation of the other. To move in only one direction is to run away, so he feels it best to run to the anonymity of the white world.

During his return home, Archilde begins to heal old wounds in preparation for his departure. He makes peace with his father, whom he has always hated, and agrees to work the family farm for one last harvest. He makes his peace with his mother, who always embarrassed him, and agrees to take her for one last hunting trip up into the mountains. He earns the respect of the old white priest and of the old Indian medicine man. By the time his mother dies, he is in a perfect position to take his place as a social leader and prosperous local rancher if he decides to stay. During the long summer at home, he has learned to live with his own limitations, the limitations of his father and mother, and most importantly, the limitations of his people. Unfortunately, his family members and friends exhibit fear, despair, and a desire to run away that drag him deep into three killings, and the book closes with Archilde becoming just another Indian gone bad.

McNickle develops a haunting image to illustrate the pessimistic dimension of his vision of Indian/white relations: Archilde's chase after an aged, wretched mare and her spring colt left out to pasture in the badlands. As he approaches to feed her some oats and clean her knotted, mud-coated tail, she runs, cherishing her freedom. The more he tries to catch her, the more she runs and resists. Intent on doing good for her and angry at her foolish independence, Archilde eventually runs her down. In the chase, she is mortally exhausted, and after accomplishing his purpose, he must shoot her and guard her worthless carcass from the coyotes. The young colt is left to itself in the badlands. Later Archilde realizes the foolishness of his actions as he muses over a similar event:

He was always forgetting that his way of seeing things was his own. His people could not understand it, but thought he was chasing after damn fool notions. All ideas were damn fool notions until they were understood and believed; and it was useless to wish them on to anybody else until the other person had come to them in the same way—by understanding and believing. (*Surrounded* 247)

As this image emphasizes, *The Surrounded* is clearly aimed at a white audience and argues that whites must understand and respect Indian cultures before they can hope that the Indians will adopt white attitudes. Whites can't do them any good by trying to force-feed them or chase them until they are dispirited. Positive cultural change can only come from a strong internal social structure, but given the historical record and the present actors, white and Indian, McNickle was not optimistic.

Yet the white audience can not help but identify with Archilde's struggle against the forces around him. Clearly his struggle gives him a virtuous quality which asserts the validity of human enterprise and raises him above those characters in the book who are totally controlled by their environment. While the world seems to let Archilde get nowhere, the reader applauds his attempt to seek meaning and happiness for himself and his people. His seeking, his awakening, take on a powerful motivational reality for both Archilde and the reader. The reader may even feel compelled to continue Archilde's struggle, in cultural terms, of course.

Runner in the Sun:
The Story of Indian Maize

McNickle's second novel was *Runner in the Sun,* published by the John Winston Company in 1954. Part of the Land of the Free series of juvenile historical fiction, it was beautifully illustrated by Apache artist and sculptor Alan Houser. In this novel, McNickle leaves the world of near insoluble contemporary problems to tell the story of a young boy from a Southwestern cliff dweller culture who is independent and intelligent, but who also has a strong desire to aid his people.

McNickle displays his storytelling ability as he perfectly grasps the conventions of this genre, skillfully blending the tensions between the young independent boy and his tradition-bound elders. The boy's ultimate task is to bring needed change to his people in a way they can accept. He must rebuff evil accusations and make a dangerous journey before he learns how to balance his individual initiatives with the good of his people. Through this theme, McNickle projects many of his own ideas about the nature of intra-cultural conflict, progress, and change.

McNickle weaves accurate anthropological detail throughout the story as he did in *They Came Here First.* Much as he dramatized the Bering Strait crossing to begin *They Came Here First,* McNickle makes the material culture and the process of agricultural change come to life in a way superior to Adolph Bandelier's less literary efforts in *The Delight Makers.* Since *Runner in the Sun* is set in the Mesa Verde period, the pre-Columbian environment enables him to draw a portrait of Indian life undisturbed by European invasion. Citing current anthropological data in his introduction, McNickle contends that though some strife existed in Native American societies, they were, on the whole, peaceful, and they respected peaceful living, especially in the Southwest. He blames

24

the European invasion for much Indian violence.

By focusing on a conflict inside the tribe, McNickle attempts to illustrate his ideas of the process of cultural change. Rival clans struggle for power, but the situation is exacerbated by a long drought that signals a changing climate and begins a new era for the people. The novelist symbolizes this cultural change through the people's desire to replace the old, weak strain of corn with a new strain, a strain that will more completely respond to the changing climate.

The world of the pueblo is one of perfect balance between culture and the land, though not an idyllic world. The change in climate and the depletion of the soil by the continual use of one strain of corn necessitate a struggle to create new forms of cultural expression. The values that the culture holds do not change, but in response to the land, the form of that cultural definition must mature to accommodate the new realities of the environment.

Socially, the pueblo is stalemated, the forces of change and the status quo unable to dominate or develop. The boy Salt's attempt to grow a new strain of corn becomes the center of controversy. He is befriended by an elder who is wise enough to question the wisdom of the ancients when conditions change. The wise elder sees that the culture and the corn are diminishing since they are too inbred and no longer adequately respond to the environment, so he sends the unselfish boy on a quest for a new strain of corn to revitalize their crops and society. After a long journey, Salt returns without the corn, feeling that he has failed in his mission. Instead, he brings a bride from another tribe and ideas about how other people live. After the elder makes him realize the value of this acquisition, the pueblo migrates south, leaving their ancestral homeland, to live happily in a fruitful, new land. Salt learns to trust the dreams of the elders, his own instincts about his new and different wife, and his desire to act for the good of his people.

In his portrayal of the conflict which ultimately brings about cultural progress, McNickle is careful to show that those who desire personal power and advantage are linked with fear and that fear begets witchcraft. To stand for the good of the people does not mean child-like obedience to tradition. It can mean finding the new and producing positive change. Of course, McNickle knew this to be true from his years of community development work, and he believed it was an idea contemporary Indian leaders needed to understand fully. In *Runner in the Sun*, the change that comes about is clearly based on a reaffirmation of cultural values brought into the open through resolution of internal dissension.

To counterpoint these images of positive change, McNickle offers a picture of the corrupt Aztec civilization flourishing on murder and domination. The Aztecs have destroyed and perverted the civilized accomplishments of their predecessors, the Mayas and other Central American groups, rather than adapting them for the good of all. At one point Salt asks, "Shouldn't a highly civilized people learn to live in peace?" Of course the Aztecs did not, but then neither did the European settlers of the Americas. Throughout this fine, young adult, historical novel, McNickle expresses timely contemporary and historical insights.

Wind from an Enemy Sky

In *Wind from an Enemy Sky*, published posthumously, McNickle again uses the situation, which he developed in *The Surrounded*, of two cultures living side by side and yet not really understanding each other's values and experience. While good intentions may exist, an essential lack of understanding and respect on both sides makes real, lasting communications and development for both peoples impossible. The whites assume an air of cultural superiority which dismisses and discounts Indian thought, culture, and values. The white idea of meeting on common ground is for the Indians to completely abandon their culture. The Indians either accept white attitudes with little thought of how they will affect Indian life, or they retreat in despair into a cultural myopia.

The state of the land is once again an indicator of the state of the cultural dynamic. As the land in the novel is literally dammed, so the natural social interaction is blocked and frustrated. In keeping with a regionalist ethic, environment and culture set the forces of plot to work. However, in this book McNickle is less naturalistic than in *The Surrounded*: his focus is not as directly on one individual's struggle against deterministic forces. The tragedy is less personal. Rather, the workings of the group's dynamic and its relation to individual volition are at the center of *Wind from an Enemy Sky*. In this novel, volition is treated as if it could be effective, if only the people involved understood the function of culture in human societies. He even presents one character, Antoine, as being in harmony with both land and culture, and thus symbolizing potential success in a way no character in *The Surrounded* does.

The book illustrates much of McNickle's historical analysis and personal experience, though in a highly dramatized manner. He places the story of the Little Elk Indians in the Montana of his youth, "I have just completed a novel, the setting for which is an Indian reservation in the Northwest—generalized from the reservation community in which I was born and the setting for an earlier novel, *The Surrounded*" (Letter to Douglas Latimer, 16 March 1976). Also, his BIA and AID experiences with the Navajos and other tribes inform the novel. After 1955, his historical books often end with an attack on federal Indian policy of the 1950s and the ever-present potential that white ignorance and exploitation could lead to mass tragedy. The novel dramatizes that potential.

In *Wind from an Enemy Sky*, the clash of cultures is not focused in one individual as it is in *The Surrounded*, but is set between two brothers on a personal level and between white and Indian on a social level. Characters represent variations on a spectrum of cultural attitudes from the uncaring progressive whites to the traditional Indian medicine man. The plot conflict revolves around two objects: a dam that cuts off a stream of Indian water which symbolizes the people's connection to the life-giving earth, and a medicine bundle which symbolizes the tribe's relation to the sacred universe. The pressures of the external society force the two brothers to respond differently to change. One brother, Henry Jim, was the leader of the tribe, but he embraces the white ways and loses the trust of his people. Though he is a prosperous rancher, he has moved off the reservation and is alienated from his people. The other brother, Bull, has been elected chief, and holds his group away from contact and cooperation with the forces that would alter traditional Indian life. A large uncommitted group has no clear leadership. Years earlier when Jim left the reservation, he turned the tribe's medicine bundle over to a local priest who in turn gave it to a foundation owned by the builder of the dam, Adam Pell. Bull is now at odds with Jim for abandoning tradition, even though Jim is seen by the white world as a model Indian capable of bridging the two worlds.

As Henry Jim ages, he returns to some tribal ways and is intent on helping his people and restoring himself to harmony with them. He convinces Bull that they must restore the medicine bundle to the people. Pell promises to return the bundle. For years he has kept it in his personal museum, but like the Indians' will and society, it has decayed. After some violence on the dam site which kills Pell's nephew, the dam builder gives the tribe not the medicine bundle but a naked, gold image created by pre-conquest Peruvian

Indians and called "the Virgin of the Andes." By that substitution, Pell hopes to replace the tribe's locus of spiritual power with something of comparable worth. The Indians' mood turns ugly as they sense another betrayal. Outraged, Bull struggles with and kills Pell and the local Indian agent. Inevitably the Indian policeman kills Bull. As in *The Surrounded*, cultural interaction has ended in death and tragedy.

In *Wind from an Enemy Sky*, McNickle minimizes the white intrusion into the social structure of much of the tribe. The tribe's internal laws and system of justice still remain intact as does its religious organization. The generations are able to connect and the community, though indecisive, retains its sense of unity.

McNickle expresses his ideas of culture and progress through the struggle between the forces for the status quo and the forces for change. In *The Surrounded*, the forces for change are identified as the white society which tries to force the Salish to accept white values, but in *Wind from an Enemy Sky* the dynamic is centered inside the tribal society as represented by the two brothers. However, the proper dynamic process is stalemated.

Although Henry Jim is living outside of any influence he may have had on his tribe, his move for reconciliation opens the way for a dialectic which will confirm culture and allow change to begin again. Unfortunately, his attempt to right his past wrongs leads to conflict with the white world, a conflict which ends in tragedy for his brother Bull and the reformist Pell. In the end, the future belongs to the young Antoine, who can understand both worlds, but who places a premium on the community's identity. Hope is left for the next generation. As McNickle wrote in a letter to anthropologist and friend Sol Tax, "Every Indian generation has to be made over in the quest for harmony. Fortunately, it always seems to work out and the community in the end remains intact;

but at great cost" (29 March 1972).

On the level of federal Indian policy, McNickle seems to be portraying the reform movement of the 1920s and 1930s which he knew well. The Indian agent Rafferty has received his position due to the new prominence of a Collier-like reform attitude in Washington. However, during the three years that he has been with the Little Elk Indians, he has yet to produce a lasting accomplishment. Yet Rafferty is willing to wait for the trust of the community and willing to give them that period for believing and understanding new ideas that McNickle sees as necessary for real change to occur.

The main problem with the reform movement is embodied in the well-meaning Adam Pell. As the architect and builder responsible for the dam which becomes the last straw of cultural violation, his attitudes are central to the story. He has assumed that the dam will directly translate into economic benefits for the Indians, but it has not. He has received the Little Elk medicine bundle for his museum in order to preserve it as an art object, but he has failed. His nephew, who works on the dam, dies because of the Indians' frustration with the state of things, and Pell is faced with the direct, personal results of his cultural assumptions.

After the killing, Pell studies the history of injustice against the Little Elk Indians, only to become appalled and outraged to see how his attempt at progress has been a further oppression of the Indians. Nevertheless, he still believes that Indians and whites can unite to create a better world, and he bases this belief on an experience he had with Peruvian Indians.

As with most social reformers, Pell's vision of a unified community is, however, based on a white view of social structure and values. This lack of understanding is symbolized by his attempt to replace the decayed medicine bundle with a stolen, pre-Incan, nude, gold statue, "Virgin of the Andes," which McNickle observes is "torn from its sociocultural setting." Clearly, McNickle is analyzing the motivation of the reformers when he has Pell take this action as a form of penance for his past sins, while groping blindly for an external "scale of values by which he could act responsibly" (214), and finally concluding with self-vindication. The tragic killings are the end result. As Rafferty so astutely observes, "because of his [Pell's] place in the world, his success, he assumed he could restore a lost world by a simple substitution of symbols" (249). Rafferty knows such "simple substitution" can not work, but McNickle implies that most social reformers do not understand this simple truth.

McNickle also implies, after his years of working between two cultures, that it is close to impossible for those cultures to truly understand and respect each other's worldviews. Rafferty says, "These people find it difficult to believe that a white man, any white man, will give them respect, as it is difficult for me to understand why they push me away and keep me from coming into their confidence. The answer, obviously, is that we do not speak to each other—and language is only part of it. Perhaps it is intention, or purpose, the map of the mind we follow" (125). Yet to the reader, all the tragedy in the novel seems so unnecessary. The white attitudes of cultural superiority leave little room for Indian responses which strengthen culture, and the reader feels that if we all could just listen and respect each other, the tragedy could be avoided. While it is clear that the application of this understanding will be no easy task, McNickle believed that too few listen and respect. He provided no easy plan of action, but he concluded that without this necessary respect and understanding, only tragedy and despair await both cultures.

III. ETHNOHISTORY

They Came Here First:
The Epic of the American Indian

They Came Here First was unique in its day. A history informed by an Indian perspective, the book was charged with insights from ethnology and molded with an understanding of cultural values. McNickle's work at the B.I.A. allowed him to do much of the research, and he compiled information from a variety of sources such as current anthropological and archaeological data, federal legislation, and reports from congressional debates. His labor resulted in an ethnohistory of the American Indian, or more precisely a history of the social interaction between whites and Indians. Throughout the book, McNickle expressed a Boasian belief in cultural relativism similar to that of the Collier administration, and he attempted to convince the reader to value and understand the perspectives of American Indian cultures. Published in 1949 as McNickle's first historical book, *They Came Here First* received very favorable notice with much enthusiasm shown by reviewers such as Clyde Kluckhohn and Stanley Vestal.

McNickle set himself numerous tasks in the book. When Collier resigned from the Bureau of Indian Affairs in 1945, the political climate turned against cross-cultural understanding. Writing in 1949, McNickle still strongly felt that the public needed to be given the most basic education about American Indians. He tried to shatter common stereotypes about Indians and Indian history. He hoped to replace the popular image of the Indian as the wild Sioux warrior à la Hollywood with more realistic images of the Hopi, Cherokee, Salish, and Iroquois so as to emphasize the variety of American Indian experience. He wanted to remind the reading public about agricultural tribes, peaceful town builders, and the developed, progressive tribal societies which existed in a delicate balance of inter-tribal relations. He knew that many readers felt Indians were primitive, barbaric, and inferior, so he reminded them of the complexity and exactitude of Indian languages; he explained how Indian concepts of law and punishment worked and remained effective even if they were different from white concepts and values; and he refuted the nineteenth-century belief in agriculture as a civilizing tool by showing that even in pre-Columbian times, agriculture did not always lead to a more progressive way of life.

This effort to explain an Indian perspective brought him to an important definition of culture: not as a static clinging to the past, but as a dynamic struggle between forces favoring the status quo and forces favoring change. He believed that solutions found inside any group reaffirmed cultural values and defined culture as a constantly developing way of life. If this dynamic were upset and overpowered, cultural deterioration took place. McNickle had covered much of the same ground in *The Surrounded*, but here his ideas were given organization and documentation.

Another important goal of the book was to draw a broad outline of Indian/white relations. McNickle closely followed the wonder and delight of both sides with the initial white/Indian contact, but then he documented the uncontrolled exploitation of the eighteenth- and nineteenth-century treaties which had resulted in so much human waste and enslavement. He recognized the wardship and reservation period as an attempt to control the exploitation, however wrongheaded and colonial the federal attitudes were. He discussed the Indian Reorganization Act of 1934 as a positive attempt to work out a final and lasting solution based on mutual respect and necessary change while still encouraging self-determination. Although he was not totally optimistic about the ultimate effect of federal legislation on American Indian experience, he saw those efforts as hopeful.

McNickle recounted the long history of misunderstanding between the two peoples, and the reader suspects that deep down McNickle felt that a culture always misunderstands another's values, thus making any solution or agreement a genuine surprise.

As he created this broad outline, McNickle strove to present this history as an exciting, if tragic, conflict. He showed the contrast between the personal actions of the Indians who met Columbus and both the wonder and the misunderstanding of the whites, as revealed in their journals. The history of Indian slavery and mass death strikes the reader with special force after McNickle's extended dramatic description of the epic struggle which the Bering Strait crossing represents and then the friendliness of the first contact between whites and Indians. He explained the reasoning behind the Indians' actions in such a way as to stir the reader's emotions, and then he contrasted it with specific statements from short-sighted politicians, military men, and bureaucrats. At the end of the book, after praising Collier's reform efforts, he warned the reader of the possibility that past misunderstandings could be repeated by nameless adversaries whom the reader must defeat in the name of respect and understanding. Through his use of dramatic structure, McNickle showed that his grasp of fiction and audience awareness served him well in non-fiction writing.

A final goal of *They Came Here First* was to support his plea for a continuation of Collier's principles in federal Indian relations. As he elaborated on misunderstandings and false expectations, McNickle implied that principles of self-determination could produce a solution. As an example of the false expectations, he cited the federal attitude, prevalent during the Dawes Act period, that farming would automatically make the Indian into a modern white man. On the other hand, Indians misunderstood, too. Reservation policy encouraged the Indian's ward attitude. The Indian felt that it was not important to farm and be independent because he would be taken care of and did not need to face the modern world. McNickle's insight into the essential mutual misunderstanding between white and Indian worldviews led him to support Collier's principles. Collier did not advocate the elimination of Indian cultures as his predecessors did; instead, he tried to use existing social organizations and cultural values to encourage attitudes which would increase tribal ability for self-determination and self-government. McNickle believed that a dynamic application of traditional values and social structures could enable Indian people to assimilate change and still reassert Indian identity. Culture and change were not incompatible but two faces of the same phenomenon, yet change must be effected by Indians in an Indian way. Even if the Indian approach was a handicap in the modern world, the Indian must have choice. Only that choice would yield rational action and, ultimately, positive results.

In 1975 McNickle brought out a revised edition of *They Came Here First*. He added chapters on the Collier years, the termination period, the surge in the sixties of Indian political awareness, and a concluding chapter. McNickle also retained much of the original text with its dramatic presentation of the material, emphasis on stereotype busting, and the explanation of Indian cultural perspectives. However, the revised edition was a greatly improved work. The style had been smoothed in some places, points expanded and clarified, and the results of the latest scholarly studies incorporated into the new text.

While much of the material in the new chapters was also presented in the revisions of *Indians and Other Americans* and *Indians of North America*, the revised *They Came Here First* stands out as the most complete statement of McNickle's insights and conclusions. In his final chapter entitled "Retrospect," McNickle discussed the lessons of power, superiority, and genocide in Indian/white relations.

He observed: "Indian society lived under the sentence of death from the first landings of an alien race. The sentence had not been pronounced in any formal proceedings and no grand strategy ever emerged. At intervals humane concern even characterized the acts of governing bodies. But the nature of the relationship was always that of executioner and victim, poised in suspense" (283). McNickle reminds the reader that the reality of cultural survival and renewal, aided by the anti-colonial attitudes of some whites and propelled by increased nationalistic Indian awareness, should bring Americans face to face with the tenets of democracy and self-determination they hold so dear. He concluded: "The possibility of such an accommodation is within reach, at remarkably little cost, and even some gain in honor and self-respect. . . . Return the right of decision to the tribes—restore their power to hold the dominant society at arm's length, and to bargain again in peace and friendship. Only by possessing such power can the tribes make useful choices within the social environment encompassing them" (285).

Indians and Other Americans: Two Ways of Life Meet

In 1959 Harper and Row published *Indians and Other Americans.* Reportedly the book had its genesis in two tours of Indian reservations by social journalist Harold Fey. Fey produced a first draft and McNickle was called in to advise and revise. The book was an interesting blend of Fey's social and humanistic activism and McNickle's historical and cultural insights. The end product, probably, reflected McNickle more than Fey, though the two men obviously agreed on its thrust.

Apparently written as a humanistic response to the Indian tragedies of the 1950s, or what McNickle later referred to as the "Eisenhower misery," the book contained sections on the post-war plight of the Navajos, the adverse results of termination, the desperation of

Indians in the cities, the debate over development of Alaskan resources, and the lamentable death of Ira Hayes from over-exposure. As with McNickle's other books, the underlying plan was to chronicle the long history of outrageous behavior on the part of whites and the federal government toward the basic human rights of the Indian tribes. The historical perspective provided a framework through which the reader could see present problems and policies.

The book's political motivation began to emerge as it explained why the wrong-headed legislation of the 1950s had made the Indian condition worse. The authors concluded with support for a proposed four-point development plan for all Indian tribes similar to the one developed for the Navajo and for Iran.

While the book had a strong chronological development and repeated some of the material from *They Came Here First*, it organized its argument around the differing appreciations whites and Indians hold of cultural concepts such as education, law, land use, sovereignty, and progress. Wanting to give the reader more than an historical understanding of white/Indian relations, the authors attempted to open the Indian perspective to white readers, to explain Indian values. Their emphasis was on the physical survival of Indian peoples, but their real aim was to reveal the survival of cultural attitudes to a modern world that barely suspected they continue, much less understood them.

In order to explain why some change was accepted and some resisted, McNickle and Fey placed change in the context of continuing cultural identity. They felt the need to combat the widespread and officially adopted notion that Indian assimilation is inevitable and imminent. This tactic put the audience of *Indians and Other Americans* into the position of asking what it could do to carry this understanding into the world around them. Fey and McNickle pointed out the folly of most previous legislative attempts to correct the "Indian problem," and they offered the concerned white reader a less doctrinaire position: "The problem then is to devise conditions and to bring to bear the stimuli which will induce Indian people to adapt their customs, attitudes, and technical skills to the necessities of life in the American community" (197). McNickle's argument was for change but for change that retained and expanded cultural identity, that remained based on self-determined needs. "To change, yet to remain steadfast—that would seem to be the need of all living things" (13).

In 1970 Harper and Row issued a revised edition of *Indians and Other Americans*. In the new edition Fey and McNickle retained most of the first edition, but changed the conclusions to some chapters, added a new introduction, and revised the concluding chapter. They reasoned that the book was still valid, since the condition of Indians had worsened since 1959. Poverty, undereducation, unemployment, and disease were still common elements of Indian life. The threat of termination and coercive assimilation still blighted efforts toward true self-determination. They concluded their new introduction by supporting the recommendations of the Kennedy Senate Subcommittee on Indian Education, which presented proposals to establish an Indian-initiated national policy to remove the "stain on our national conscience."

In the new concluding chapter, the authors evaluated the changes that had taken place in the sixties. They saw two trends that clearly emerged in those socially active and politically publicized times. First, they saw a growth in pan-tribal cooperation, a subject that would increasingly inform McNickle's later ethnohistorical writings. The culturally aware war veterans and the new, vocal, politically active youths such as those in the National Indian Youth Council, perceived a need to join with other Indians to present a united front to federal and state governments in an effort to redress wrongs and assure their rights. Tracing the concept back to the National Congress of American Indians, the two authors lauded the development of an identity that was Indian as opposed to only Sioux or Navajo.

Second, echoing McNickle's experience with the BIA and AID, the authors placed an increased emphasis on their conviction that action must be initiated from within the community, no matter how well planned or well intended the outside help might be. They cited the positive results of community-initiated projects in education, legal services, and economic opportunity. In these progressive changes, the authors saw some hope, some promise. They believed that, at last, Indian people were becoming more vocal and beginning to demand the fulfillment of centuries of promises.

Indian Tribes of the United States:
Ethnic and Cultural Survival

In 1962 Oxford University Press published *Indian Tribes of the United States* as part of the London Institute of Race Relations series. In the small book McNickle reviewed much of the federal Indian policy that made up *They Came Here First*, but this time the chronicle was informed with an insight into the way Indian resistance to white cultural assumptions could be seen as a coherent expression of Indian personality and culture.

McNickle was again interested in busting stereotypes. While attempting to define who an Indian is, McNickle wanted to destroy both the image of the vanishing American, becoming assimilated into modern American culture and the image of the sullen, ignorant savage, who was too dumb to appreciate the fruits of progress being offered to him. Behind the Indian resistance to white domination was a culture surviving, and with Indian populations on the rise, McNickle stressed that modern America had to understand and work with these cultures if further tragedy were to be avoided.

In the thirteen years between the publication of *They Came Here First* and *Indian Tribes of the United States*, McNickle had improved his historical knowledge of Indian/white relations: his sections on early colonial policy of the Spanish and English were much fuller and more completely documented, and his explanation of the Marshal era followed the struggle between congressional forces and public attitudes with an eye toward emphasizing the popular perceptions of Indians. He explored Indian motivation behind the signing of the treaties and the reasons why the federal government and popular opinion moved away from treaty relations with the tribes into a reservation system.

As always McNickle tried to explain Indian values concerning law, land, and social structure, but the new material in the book was his discussion of Collier's initiative of cultural relativity as a path toward encouraging cultural survival. Treating tribes as operating municipalities with limited sovereignty allowed the tribes the potential for social and political action on a community level, while providing them a toehold in the modern American political superstructure. While some necessary white values like majority rule may have been at first divisive, the political structure encouraged eventual agreement and action. McNickle's years with the Crownpoint citizenship project proved that he was positive about the possibility of Indians developing political and social initiatives on the local level, yet his creation and support of the National Congress of American Indians demonstrated that he also knew that pan-tribal political awareness was needed on the national level.

His praise of the Collier years, of course, prepared the way for an attack on the fifties policies of termination and relocation. In *Indian Tribes of the United States*, McNickle situated those policies in reference to the broader political climate of a backlash against Big Government and a states' rights sentiment which influenced the public and the government in the early 1950s. With statistical precision, he recounted the devastating effects of termination on the Klamath and the Menominee. McNickle explained that Indian tribes didn't want to be dependent and didn't acknowledge any inferiority, but except for a few harried years, there had been no effective federal help which allowed them to retain their cultural identity and also offered a bridge to the modern world. His argument emphasized that people are slow to change and will only change when the cultural dynamic is allowed to work freely. He concluded the book with a passage from the "Declaration of Indian Purpose," which he helped author. The document, adopted by a body of 500 Indian leaders at a Chicago conference, read: "In short, the Indians ask for assistance, technical and financial, however long that may be, to regain in the America of the space age some measure of the adjustment they enjoyed as the original possessors of their native land" (*Tribes* 67).

The book was expanded, revised, and reissued by Oxford under the title *Native American Tribalism: Indian Survivals and Renewals* in 1973. McNickle added more completely developed factual data, new chapter summaries, and many pictures of contemporary Indians in both traditional and modern situations. Also included was expanded material from his revised *Indians and Other Americans* on the disastrous results of termination for the tribes as well as documentation of encouraging signs of self-determination in the Navajo.

In the new preface, McNickle praised the positive effects of Indian activism even if some Indian actions were naive, impatient, and divisive. In a letter to a white group distraught about a disruption by Indian demonstrators, he wrote, "Your experience of last summer is by no means an isolated instance of militancy exhibited by protesting young Indians and it should be understood, not as rowdyism, but as a kind of delayed reaction to generations of cultural suppression. Underneath it is an earnest though not always well directed search for identity and a proper place in contemporary society" (Letter to Mr. Scott, 28 January 1972). In *Native American Tribalism*, McNickle struggled, as he did in his letter to Mr. Scott, to make clear the background of despair and frustration that created the 1972 takeover of the BIA offices in Washington and the 1973 confrontation at Wounded Knee. In analyzing the politicized interactions of the 1960s and 1970s, McNickle took the long historical view, seeing the activity as fitful attempts to collect long overdue promissory notes. While obliquely critical of the American Indian Movement position, he asserted that these events challenge common white assumptions about Indians and what is good for them. Since activism had produced pan-tribal political initiatives and legislative attempts at improvements, McNickle concluded that it was now up to the government to show Indian communities that they need not riot to create the conditions for fruitful action.

Two new chapters reinforced *Native American Tribalism*. McNickle's experience as a professor at the University of Saskatchewan had given him access to regional government documents and an opportunity to increase his knowledge of the history of Canadian Indian policy. In one chapter, he reviewed the history of the Indian/Canadian interaction and presented a critique of proposed Canadian legislation which, in 1969, like American termination policy of the 1950s, had threatened to nullify treaty rights and withdraw federal support. McNickle described with relish the pan-tribal offensive to defeat the legislation and concluded that Canadian Indians were learning the lessons of pan-tribal political action and self-determination.

A second chapter reviewed federal Indian policy as it related to the Native American groups of Alaska. Here too he described successful pan-tribal organizing which defeated attempted encroachment on tribal lands.

In his conclusion, McNickle praised the political, social, and artistic achievements of Indians during the sixties. His mood was one of guarded optimism and of great cultural pride. He hoped that this new explosion of cultural reaffirmation and social awareness would educate and sustain all involved so that in the coming years, Indian self-determination and white tolerance would expand. This new effort, McNickle thought, "may prove to be the decisive force in bringing into being an enduring policy of self-determined cultural pluralism" (*Tribalism* 169).

Indian Man: A Life of Oliver La Farge

The idea of a book on La Farge was suggested to McNickle by Indiana University Press, which in 1971 published McNickle's *Indian Man*. During his many years with the BIA, McNickle had known and respected the noted writer and Indian advocate. Indeed, La Farge had given McNickle's novel *The Surrounded* its most favorable and most visible review in *The Saturday Evening Post*. Until La Farge died in 1963, the two authors occasionally had worked together on Indian projects and in Indian rights organizations, particularly with the 1940 Inter-American conference which had considered the problems of all Indians of North America, and in the Association for American Indian Affairs. Yet theirs was not a close relationship. "I could never get excited about the guy (my long acquaintance with him never ripened into any kind of comaraderie) . . ." (Letter to John Warner, 12 November 1971).

Despite his lack of personal engagement, McNickle's biography was a sensitive, appreciative look at a man who, though coming from an upper class background, was still capable of understanding and valuing the complexities of American Indian life. During a youthful journey through the Southwest, La Farge had come face to face with an alien culture with values completely different from those of his accepted way of life. He forced himself to evaluate his own culture, and he began to see that behind the apparent simplicity of Indian culture existed a rich and vital human depth.

After this initial cross-cultural experience, La Farge slowly began to dedicate himself to the study of anthropology, especially Indian cultures. McNickle chronicled La Farge's change from an unsure escapist adventurer to a man of deep social and cultural commitment. Though McNickle thought La Farge still carried too many of his parlor manners into his relations with Indians, he fully developed how La Farge had become a self-sufficient Westerner, able to move away from the contemporary wisdom, which called for total Indian assimilation, to an understanding that change need not mean cultural destruction. In a letter to Professor Omer Stewart on 28 January 1972, McNickle wrote:

> The man's career was curiously incomplete. He rejected the role of the complete gentleman, for which his upbringing prepared him; failed to stay with ethnology, for which he seemed to have a natural affinity; was thwarted in his efforts to write serious literature by the demands on his time; and devoted himself, exclusively at times, to doing good works for Indians, for which the rewards could never be commensurate with the effort. He realized this with growing poignancy in his later years. It was a difficult experience to describe.

To explain this curious mixture of broken promise and great dedication, McNickle tried to capture what he saw as an essential juxtaposition of characteristics which united La Farge's personality, a man who held East Coast Brahmin attitudes toward many things and who, at times, thought of himself as a patron to the Indians. This was the intellectual who believed in Indian survival and theories of cultural relativism, who searched for "a practical application of social sciences to the problems of Indian affairs administration" (91). On the other hand, there was the man who could sit all night with the Apaches and let their insights form his policy or could live for eight days out of provisions carried on a pack horse. McNickle struggled as he wrote the book, "the LaFarge job has got me completely swamped, and I find myself admiring a man whom in the flesh I found difficult to take. His was a thorny exterior" (Letter to Royal Hassrick, 16 March 1969).

As he searched for resolution of these paradoxical qualities, McNickle came closer to an appreciation of La Farge's internal struggle. La Farge's commitment was, on the one hand, a personal one, one reflective of the longing for dedication and spirit which Oliver always felt he had inherited from his artistic grandfather. McNickle saw that longing at the center of La Farge's existence:

He [La Farge] once wrote: "When I look in my own memory for the essences of what I've so loved in Indian camps, the summation of it, I find a tricky rhythm tapped out on a drum, a clear singing voice, and the sound of laughter."

When he was close to the strange power of utterance and could feel himself stretching to encompass it, he was deeply satisfied, as if he had arrived at a sought for destination. It was only when he was away from it, in a moment of introspection, that the effort seemed unreal. His breeding caught up with him then and reminded him of lessons learned and obligations natural to his learning. Reason cautioned him that he had no business trying to escape from what he was born to be. His dilemma was real, a constant companion. He could not be Indian; he did not want to be submerged in the power class of his generation. (69)

On the other hand, La Farge's search was not uncommon to those members of "The Lost Generation" who saw a familiar, orderly world tossed apart and sought meaning in individualistic and often anti-modern ways. For a boy of refined Harvard tastes, the American West seemed to be a throw-back, something primitive and raw, yet true. As McNickle observed, "The truth is leaner in the West" (235). The West showed La Farge a directness of communication that his culture had lost. The West at the time seemed to lack history and maturity, and La Farge, as an archaeologist and organizer, could help supply both. "He was determined to be a good Westerner" (236) because it was in the West, especially after he had settled in Santa Fe, that La Farge could balance the conflict of sophisticated sensibilities and primitive spirit and potential.

The above quote not only expresses McNickle's understanding of La Farge, but it also reveals McNickle's personality. It seems likely that McNickle could see his own position, to some extent, in a reversal of La Farge's position. McNickle seems to have spent years avoiding what he was born to be. His years in Europe and New York must have constantly brought him back to look at "lessons and obligations natural to his learning." La Farge may have struck McNickle as a mirror image of himself, a double moving from the white world to the Indian as McNickle had moved from the Indian to the white. Both existed somewhere between, trying to be true to their origins, yet trying to participate in the other world—both of them confident about the value of cultural relativism and mutual respect, yet at times despairing of its true flowering. McNickle's complete dedication to Indian work after 1936 may have been his way of resolving his own dilemma. About La Farge, McNickle wrote, "I still don't like his attitude toward Indians, in spite of what he accomplished on their behalf and the undoubted sacrifices his Indian work required of him. He seems never to have acquired humility, which is always a great lack in a human being. But he was fearless, faithful and a hell of a hard worker. One can settle for that" (Letter to Pam Cragun, 15 February 1969). While McNickle never wrote his autobiography, some of his self-understanding is expressed in what he wrote about Oliver La Farge.

To piece together this puzzle of East and West, Indian and white, a puzzle which existed in La Farge, McNickle had to explain the psychology of life between two cultures. Although he was fascinated by the task, it would not have been enough to sustain his work on the biography if he had not seen in the book a chance to write a history of Indian Affairs over an important thirty-year period. He confided that he "persisted with the biography largely because of my interest in writing the history of Indian affairs during the period from the 1920s through the Eisenhower years" (Letter to John Warner, 12 November 1971).

La Farge's Indian work covered the period from just before Collier's commissionership to the late 1950s. Since La Farge was at the center of much of the political struggle during that period, McNickle could delineate La Farge's contributions at the same time that he chronicled the changing national policy. Through a discussion of the influence of one key individual, he could analyze the effects of Indian Rights organizations as well as the influence of anthropology and the social sciences on federal Indian policy. While McNickle had immense personal experience in these areas, the focus of his ethnohistories had not allowed him ample scope to document these aspects of modern Indian affairs. So the La Farge biography offered him a chance to write that history from a personal and more subjective viewpoint.

The reviews for *Indian Man* were, on the whole, favorable. One

47

critic observed that McNickle wrote about La Farge with dignity and respect. But the book did not seem to generate much interest. McNickle referred to it hitting the market with a "dull thud." Some reviewers complained that the book was more of a history than a biography. As McNickle had expected, "Reviewers seem not to be satisfied with a biography unless you undress your subject in public and call attention to his imperfections" (Letter to Morris Burge, 13 March 1972). Though he concluded the book would probably find favor only with a specialized audience, he was pleased with his contribution to the understanding of La Farge and modern Indian policy, and he knew he was justified in his approach to La Farge because Indian affairs had become the essence of Oliver La Farge's life as they had of his own.

IV. CONCLUSION

In a letter supporting the University of Colorado's award of an honorary doctorate to McNickle, noted ethnologist Alexander Leighton wrote:

> He has been productive as both creative writer and historian, but his essence is educator in the broadest, deepest, and truest sense of the word. His outstanding ability to combine scholarship, reflections, originality and action have [sic] been selflessly dedicated in life-long service to human beings caught in the obstacles and tragedies imposed by a rapidly changing world. This has taken practical form in his work for the American Indian. He is a modest man who lets what he does speak for him. (Letter to Omer Stewart, 27 January 1966)

Almost everything that McNickle wrote was directly concerned with the tragic interface between two cultures. But he wrote as an educator, to encourage understanding, both self-understanding and cross-cultural understanding. As Alfonso Ortiz has written: "Indeed, if D'Arcy lived for anything, he lived to reduce that awful strangeness which has for so long separated Indian and white on this hemisphere" ("Across" 16). While he was not naive about the extent of his success, McNickle was sure progress could be made and at least some potential tragedy could be avoided. McNickle, as an Indian intellectual with vast experience in the white world, was ideally suited to speak to both worlds. Not only was he in the right position, but he possessed the necessary qualities of empathy and analysis, reverence and articulateness to face problems and define Indian identity in terms that white society could understand. He could see Indian society with white eyes and white society with Indian eyes, or as Lawrence Towner has written, ". . . he was both totally Indian and totally 'European' " (*Surrounded* 302).

McNickle professed cultural pluralism long before it was popular. When it was just a theory of the social sciences, it was a creed for him, one he was constantly pushing white America to adopt. All of his written work is one vast, constantly evolving argument for a unified vision of cultural relativism and continuing cultural identity for Native Americans. Yet for McNickle, culture was not defined by what could be hidden, preserved, kept unchanged, and isolated from the future. His vision was dynamic. In a discussion of the disappearance of the Eskimos, he wrote:

> There is no question but that Eskimo life is changing and
> will continue to trend away from the style of life they have
> known. What will disappear will be the Eskimo of, say, 1900,
> but it was never preordained that Eskimo life would attain
> some climax and become fossilized. The most notable feature
> of man is his adaptability. (Letter to Cheryl Moyer, 5 July 1971)

He believed that culture was defined dialectically as the struggle between the forces for the status quo and the forces for change. Culture, thus, was the mechanism by which the conflict was resolved, the means for defining identity and continuity. He was in a position to and had the ability to bring his opinions to a wide audience. Consequently, he held an important position in a larger and continuing intercultural debate. As Alfonso Ortiz put it, "D'Arcy struck one theme, well worthy of reflection, throughout the last four decades of his life. He observed that, despite what seemed on the surface to be massive and rapid breakdown in Indian cultures across the continent, an essential core of cultural integrity was being maintained" ("Obituary" 633). A culture was defined by the qualities it used to assimilate change. McNickle knew American Indian cultures must change; indeed, they always had. But change must not wipe out identity; it must reaffirm it. Whatever tragedies and hardships Indian peoples suffered during McNickle's time, they had always recreated themselves around a core of cultural identity which, though different, was uniquely Indian. "D'Arcy was one of only a handful of scholars who knew this would always be so, and he knew this because it was his own story that he was telling" (Ortiz, "Across" 16).

Perhaps the most influential role that McNickle played was as the grandfather of modern Indian nationalism. He realized that if positive change were to come, Indians must have their hands on the steering wheel, and as an organizer and advocate of pan-tribal activism, he held a great appeal for a younger generation of Indian leaders who saw both his command of contemporary affairs and the integrity of his Indian identity. McNickle's lead has been followed by a generation of Indian writers and activists who have tried to duplicate his combination of profound insight and artistic mastery. While appreciated as the first modern American Indian novelist, he is also highly praised for voicing a strong Indian perspective in his fiction and non-fiction.

Though McNickle's fiction was out of print for most of the Indian renaissance during the late sixties and seventies, his ethnohistorical work was not. In it he presented a world of coherent Indian values which could be contrasted to the dominant culture. All of his writing also praised the pan-tribal sense of nationalism from which young Indian artists and leaders were drawing strength. His personal influence was great among the emerging college-trained and politically aware as he touched many of their lives through the John Whitney Hays foundation grants, the National Congress of American Indians, the summer workshop for Indian youth, and numerous other activist projects. Alfonso Ortiz pointed out that he left behind "a host of Indian leaders and younger scholars inspired by the example of his varied works of service to the diverse peoples of America" ("Obituary" 634).

Moreover, McNickle's fiction has inspired contemporary American Indian authors. People learned of his novels, but had to hunt them down through libraries. Yet clearly, N. Scott Momaday and especially James Welch owe something to his vision of the reservation and the clash of cultures. Momaday writes, "I have no doubt that D'Arcy McNickle's example was very important to Native American writers of the 60s and 70s. It was a crucial time for examples, and D'Arcy through his work stood in the right place at the right time" (Letter to the author, 1 April 1986). Acoma writer Simon Ortiz recently honored McNickle by titling his new anthology of Native American fiction, *Earth Power Coming*, from a line in *Wind from an Enemy Sky*. Simon Ortiz has written about the ways in which the climate of social-political activism was important in his writing and the work of other writers such as Leslie Silko and Vine Deloria. Writers were looking for models, and while there was little tradition of written American Indian literature, these writers found in the work of Charles Eastman and D'Arcy McNickle some tradition of intellectual Indian writers to inspire them.

Although critics such as Charles Larson and Louis Owens have centered their discussion of McNickle's fiction on the vision of despair and tragedy, much criticism remains to be produced which explores the literary and ethnohistorical context of his fiction. Historically, *The Surrounded* fits neatly into our current understandings of American novels of the thirties with their social questionings of the inevitability and correctness of American progress and the American dream. But more deeply his fiction grows out of the tradition of American Naturalism and represents a regionalism in keeping with the work of other writers such as Mary Austin, Eudora Welty, and Willa Cather who were exploring the societies and cultures of American regions. Of equal importance is the balance that McNickle's fiction adds to white views of Indian life presented by writers such as Frank Waters, Oliver La Farge, William Eastlake, and Adolph Bandelier. As our literary understanding of the first half of the twentieth century becomes more complete, our appreciation of D'Arcy McNickle will grow. As the present emphasis on literary studies of contemporary American Indian fiction widens, the interest in *Wind from an Enemy Sky* will grow because the novel both continues McNickle's earlier concerns and responds to contemporary American Indian literature.

As more white Americans learn of the literary traditions of minorities, McNickle's reputation and influence increase. Already *The Surrounded*, reissued by the University of New Mexico Press, has found an infinitely wider audience than it did in 1936, and *Wind from an Enemy Sky* is popular reading on many campuses. As more readers discover this man of insight and humanity, perhaps a little more tolerance and understanding will come into the world—a fitting tribute to a remarkable man.

Selected Bibliography

WORKS BY McNICKLE

Indians and Other Americans: A Study of Indian Affairs. Co-authored by Harold Fey. 1959; rpt. New York: Harper, 1970.

The Indian Tribes of the United States: Ethnic and Cultural Survival. 1962; rpt. as *Native American Tribalism: Indian Renewals and Survivals.* New York: Oxford UP, 1973.

Indian Man: A Life of Oliver La Farge. Bloomington: Indiana UP, 1971.

Runner in the Sun: The Story of Indian Maize. New York: Winston, 1954, rpt. Albuquerque: U of New Mexico P, 1987.

The Surrounded. New York: Dodd-Mead, 1936; rpt. U of New Mexico P, 1978.

They Came Here First: the Epic of the American Indian. New York: Lippincott, 1949; rpt. New York: Octagon, 1975.

Wind from an Enemy Sky. New York: Harper, 1978.

SELECTED ARTICLES:

"American Indians Who Never Were," First Convocation of American Indian Scholars. Princeton University, 1970. *New University Thought* 7.3 (1971): 24-29.

"Americans Called Indians." *North American Indians in Historical Perspective.* Ed. Leacock and Lurie. New York: Random, 1971. 29-63.

"Basis for a National Indian Policy." *The American Indian* 5.1 (1949): 3-12.

"The Healing Vision." *Tomorrow* 4.3 (1956): 25-31.

"The Indian in American Society." *Minority Groups: Segregation and Integration.* Papers of the 82nd Annual Forum of the National Conference of Social Work. New York: Columbia UP, 1955. 68-77.

"It Takes Two to Communicate." Co-authored by Viola Pfrommer. *International Journal of Health Education* 2.3 (1959): 136-41.

"John Collier's Vision." Editorial. *The Nation* 3 June 1968: 718-19.

"Peyote and the Indian." *Scientific Monthly* 57 (1943): 220-29.

"Private Intervention." *Human Organization* 20 (1961-62): 208-15.

"A U.S. Indian Speaks." *Americas* 6.3 (1954): 8-11 + .

"The Sociocultural Setting of Indian Life." *American Journal of Psychiatry* 125.2 (1968): 115-19.

MAJOR PUBLISHED SHORT STORIES

"Meat for God." *Esquire* Sept. 1935: 86 + .

"Snowfall." *Common Ground* 4.4 (1944): 75-82.

"Train Time." *Scholastic* 24 Oct. 1936: 13-14.

WORKS CITED AND OTHER
MATERIAL CONCERNING McNICKLE

Colonnese, Tom, and Louis Owens. *American Indian Novelists: An Annotated Critical Bibliography.* New York: Garland, 1985. 25-30.

Hans, Birgit. "The Hawk is Hungry: An Annotated Anthology of D'Arcy McNickle's Short Fiction." M.A. Thesis. U of Arizona, 1986.

La Farge, Oliver. Rev. of *The Surrounded. Saturday Review of Literature* 14 Mar. 1936: 10.

Larson, Charles. *American Indian Fiction.* Albuquerque: U of New Mexico P, 1978. 68-78.

Oakes, Priscilla. "The First Generation of Native American Novelists." *Multi-Ethnic Literatures of the United States* 5.1 (1978): 57-65.

Oakes (Shames), Priscilla. "The Long Hope: A Study of American Indian Stereotypes in American Popular Fiction, 1890-1950." Diss. U of California at Los Angeles, 1969. 221-29.

Ortiz, Alfonso. "D'Arcy McNickle (1904-1977) Across the River and Up the Hill: a Personal Remembrance." *American Indian Journal* 4.4 (1978): 12-16. Rpt. as "Obituary: D'Arcy McNickle, 1904-1977." *American Anthropologist* 81 (1979): 632-36.

Ortiz, Simon. "Toward a National Indian Literature: Cultural Authenticity in Nationalism." *Multi-Ethnic Literatures of the United States* 8.2 (1981): 7-12.

Owens, Louis. "The 'Map of the Mind': D'Arcy McNickle and the American Indian Novel." *Western American Literature* 19 (1984): 275-83.

Wiget, Andrew. *Native American Literature*. Boston: Twayne, 1985. 77-82, 94-5.

All letters and diaries cited in the text are in the D'Arcy McNickle Collection, The Newberry Library, Chicago, Illinois.